CW00894490

Find Your Mantra

Inspire and Empower Your Life with 75 Positive Affirmations

Aysel Gunar

Founder of

Dedication: To my children.

Brimming with creative inspiration, how-to projects, and useful information to enrich your everyday life, Quarto Knows is a favorite destination for those pursuing their interests and passions. Visit our site and dig deeper with our books into your area of interest: Quarto Creates, Quarto Cooks, Quarto Homes, Quarto Lives, Quarto Drives, Quarto Explores, Quarto Gifts, or Quarto Kids.

First published in 2019 by Rock Point,
an imprint of The Quarto Group
142 West 36th Street, 4th Floor
New York, NY 10018, USA
T (212) 779-4972 F (212) 779-6058
www.QuartoKnows.com

10 9 8 7 6 5 4 3 2

ISBN: 978-1-63106-622-1

Editorial Director: Rage Kindelsperger
Creative Director: Laura Drew
Managing Editor: Cara Donaldson
Senior Editor: John Foster
Development Editor: Leeann Moreau
Art Director: Cindy Samargia Laun
Cover Design: Emily Weigel
Page Design: Amy Harte

Library of Congress Cataloging-in-Publication Data

Names: Gunar, Aysel, author.
Title: Find your mantra : inspire and empower your life
with 180 positive affirmations / Aysel Gunar.
Description: New York: Rock Point, an imprint of The Quarto Group, 2019.
Identifiers: LCCN 2019015773 | ISBN 9781631066221
Subjects: LCSH: Affirmations. | Mantras. | Mindfulness (Psychology) | Optimism.
Classification: LCC BF697.5.S47 G78 2019 | DDC 158.1—dc23
LC record available at https://lccn.loc.gov/2019015773

Printed in China

Contents

Introduction

I started MantraBand® in 2012, as a way to remind myself to be more present and worry less. Inspired by my son, who was two years old at the time, I wanted to be present and "live in the moment," just like him. I thought a bracelet with the words "Live in the Moment" would serve as the perfect reminder. As someone who rarely wore jewelry, I felt the bracelet needed to be simple and the material very durable. When I couldn't find one that I liked, I decided to design my own. What started with only five mantras is now a collection of 150+ mantras meant to inspire and empower every day.

MantraBand® bracelets are simple, elegant, and timeless pieces that are meant to be worn every day and last a lifetime. After the bracelets have served their function, many of our customers like to pass them on to a person who may need the message. In addition to the bracelet, each MantraBand® comes with an inspirational message that explains the meaning behind the mantra. For years, our customers have told us that these messages are meaningful to them and that they like to keep them in their wallets or on their desks in order to reflect and be inspired.

In this book, I have collected our most popular mantras, inspirational messages, benefits, and action items to help inspire you, too. Whenever you need an uplifting or encouraging reminder, just flip through the following pages, or simply open to a random page and be guided. *Find Your Mantra* continues our mission to transform lives through the power of positive words and affirmations by using meaningful words on which to meditate, inspire, and bring insight into your day-to-day life to empower your dreams. Now that you know a little about me and MantraBand®, on to some interesting mantra facts.

In their traditional Buddhist and Hindu roots, mantras are phrases that are repeated during meditation or chanted in groups to bring awareness out of a person's physical body and into a higher spiritual plane. While there are many different cultures and practices that surround mantras, Vedic or Sanskrit mantras could possibly be the oldest, dating back at least 3000 CE. When these Vedic hymns are chanted, their unique vibrations and musicality are believed to make the chanter themselves vibrate with the special frequency of that hymn, and in doing so, they find deeper meaning outside of their translations.

You will not find Vedic chants in this book, as the mantras included here are more modern and would not be considered a chant, per se, but more as pieces of a formula for a fulfilling life. These mantras also come by many other names: prayers, hymns, mottos, cornerstones, catchphrases, and slogans, just to name a few.

Mantras like these are tools; when we indulge in destructive thoughts, as humans are known to do on occasion, we can build up a deeper negativity bias. By encouraging this negativity, we put a damper on the bright light that wants to grow within each of us. If we let our minds wander toward destructive thoughts, they will proliferate. Inviting positive mantras into your daily routines flexes the most optimistic parts of your brain. By changing the way you think, you'll change the way you feel. If you're feeling optimistic and opportunistic, you'll find that the road will rise up to meet you.

Short, sweet, and to the point, the mantras you find within these pages start with the special message our customers so dearly love, followed by an action and benefit of how to incorporate them into your life. If you're not sure which of the mantras sing to you just yet, read a little more about how others interpret them and see if empathy and warmth bloom within you. Perhaps you already know the type of energy you want to bring into your life but are unsure of the steps to take? The actions are cues that can bring these mantras out of your cerebral experience and into the real world. Journal about your journey, meditate on what you learned, and actively participate in the new joy that you're looking to bring about in your life. Hopefully, by bringing these mantras into your heart, you'll reap the benefits of the outcome. These little reminders are already intrinsic truths that you know at your core. By repeating them and incorporating them into your daily life, you'll just bring this deeper awareness to the forefront of your being. You know that you should be kind to yourself, that you are a powerhouse, and that the universe supports you, but sometimes you just need a reminder.

Mantras and meditations are tools for thought so that you can rebuild the way you think if the way you think isn't working for you. While you are learning how to wield these tools, be kind to yourself. Gently guide your thoughts to where you want them to be; retraining your mind will be slow at first, but with patience and repetition, you will surely pull through. These tools will help you construct your perfect "mind palace" and share your light with the people you cherish.

Mantras alone will not get you to your big goal, a greater spiritual connection to the universe, a fancy car, or love of your life, but they will put you in the right mindset to seek out that which will serve your best self. If your best self includes any of the things mentioned above, some form of them will come to you.

Find love in your heart for yourself and love for just about everything else will follow.

Peace

Everything will be alright.

Breathe, let go, and trust that everything always unfolds perfectly and just as you need it to. Focus on the present moment and live in the now. Know that everything will be alright.

Mantra Action:

The dark is greedy, but you are bright. During meditations (or just when times are tough) flutter the eyelids closed. Elongate your neck and tilt your chin ever so slightly toward the sky. Find the sun in the dark. Everything will be alright.

Mantra Benefit:

Tough times are sticky and pervasive. Once you have peace in your heart, you can seek refuge there. The act of lifting your chin opens your heart and allows in more light.

Gratitude.

The Buddha thought that desire was the root of all suffering. By that logic, wouldn't gratitude then be the root of all happiness and peace? Once we find contentment and joy in the smallest of things, the world transforms into a garden of possibility. Be thankful and share your gratitude with those around you. Gratitude is a gift that keeps giving. Count your blessings and you'll find that they are numerous. Express gratitude and live by it, because gratitude brings peace and happiness and turns what you have into enough. Know that you will have more of what you are grateful for.

Mantra Action:

On your birthday, make a list of people, experiences, feelings, relationships, and anything else you can think of that you are thankful for—as many as the age you're turning. Making this an annual, simple exercise will ensure that not a year goes by when you don't sit down and appreciate all the things in life that bring you joy. If compiling a year's worth of thanks into one day seems daunting, start small by gratitude journaling from day to day or even week to week.

Mantra Benefit:

When you look at each passing year with an eye for gratitude, you'll get better and better at it until the number of things you're thankful for greatly outnumbers the years that you've been on this beautiful earth.

MIND

OVER

MATTER.

The brain is a beautiful thing. It's deeply complex and intricate with so many neural pathways that it's hard to know exactly which electrical impulses are being fired from where. Remember that you are the master of your mind. Know that you can and will accomplish all that you set out to do if you just believe that you can do it.

Mantra Action:

Changing your life comes from changing your thoughts. Set the pace for your new brain space. While you're falling asleep each night, imagine what the best possible version of yourself will do tomorrow. Send affirmations into your dreams filled with all of the things that you are capable of and deserve. Reaffirm your worth in the mirror the following morning to set your mood for the day. You are strong. You are capable. Your life will be filled with all of the joy, delight, and fulfilment that you wish for yourself.

Mantra Effect:

Eventually you'll start believing that all the wonderful things about you are real. Confidence is the key to success, and you just need to unlock it.

NO REGRETS

You live and learn. You grow and move on. Focus on the choices you make today. Love deeply and forgive quickly. Live on purpose, be yourself, and be kind. Take chances, make mistakes, and learn from them. Or make mistakes to be really certain that that a particular path is not meant for you. No great growth has ever come from quietly working in the secure margins. Follow your dreams. Say, "Yes!" and not "Yeah, but..." Let yourself wildly color outside the lines. Your life is a beautiful masterpiece. It is not meant to be quelled.

Mantra Action:

Remove the word "mistake" from your vocabulary. You no longer mess up; you only open yourself up to opportunities for learning and growth. You only participate in "happy accidents." Welcome the wrong because from the foulest compost comes the most beautiful flowers.

Mantra Benefit:

The life you lead will not be without a touch of suffering, but if you know in your heart of hearts that the suffering was worth the "yes!" you committed to, you will no longer experience the "what ifs?" that accompany an unfulfilled life.

All I need is within me.

You are a seed. A well. A house.
You are everything you are searching for.
You have all you need to create what you want, to do what you want, and to be the best version of yourself.

Mantra Action:

Remember that whatever the circumstances are, all you need to get through is inside of you. Have courage, face your fears, persevere. There is nothing you cannot do if you only believe and act upon it. You're already complete, but don't be afraid to push the boundaries of your existence.

Mantra Benefit:

When you stop seeking fulfillment and meaning from outside of yourself, you'll be able to reach new magnificent heights. When you know that you have all it takes to make it happen, you will be more confident in your decisions and actions. With less time spent searching for what you need, you'll have the mental capacity to find new acts that bring more delight into your life.

Everything happens for a reason.

The purpose may be hidden, but deep in your heart you know this is the path you should be on right now. Every single step is carrying you along your journey with lessons to learn, to grow, and to become who you are meant to be.

Mantra Action:

Pick a book you haven't read. Flip to a page in the middle and read a paragraph. Does it make sense? Perhaps, but it is likely out of context. Each experience (beautiful or otherwise) is a single smudge on the impressionist painting that is your life. You won't be able to see the final outcome until it's done.

Mantra Benefit:

Peace can be found when you stop trying to control every aspect of your life. If you believe, truly believe, that everything happens for a reason, being fluid and adaptable will become second nature.

LIVE
MORE.
WORRY
LESS.

Why worry? When you worry about something, you suffer it twice. Live more mindfully, fearlessly, and with an open heart. Be present in this moment. Practice gratitude and trust the journey that it leads you on. Let your "what ifs" be positive rather than the worst possible outcome. Enjoy the experience and only problem-solve when there's an actual problem.

Mantra Action:

An effective meditation for calming persistent fretting is to inhale the word "let" and exhale the word "go." Sit with this meditation. Nurse it for a while if you're prone to worry. It'll ease the current crop of concerns and calm new ones before they take root.

Mantra Benefit:

Using this meditation over time, you'll feel your shoulders relax down your back. Rolling back your shoulders opens your heart, which will in turn lead you toward the future, instead of staying trapped and guarded behind the wall of your rib cage.

Peace.
Love.
Happiness.

Remember that the real source of peace, love, and happiness is within you. Bring peace, give love, give back, and you will experience more peace, love, and happiness in your life.

Mantra Action:

Peace in your life comes from peace of mind. Meditate on the things that bring a sense of calm and meaning to your life. Love is done best when you embrace an unconditional love for yourself. Find little ways to love yourself every day, so as not to lose the pieces of you that you cherish most. Happiness can be found in the most mundane places. Practice self-care, make more jokes, drink water, start each day with a made bed or a clean sink, go out, stay in, and do whatever little things make you smile, however bizarre, quirky, or normal they may seem.

Mantra Benefit:

Creating a sense of calm and joy from within means that you won't have to rely on any outside influences to make each day a great one. When you tap that well of peace, love, and happiness at the core of yourself, you can bring it to the people, places, and work around you that you treasure.

SMILE,
BREATHE,
AND
GO
SLOWLY

These simple words are the foundation of a happy, calm, and fulfilled existence. Remember to focus on one thing at a time and give each and every moment your all. Stay calm, look on the bright side, and keep going. Because it's all about the journey, not the destination. Move at your own pace and don't compare your journey to that of others.

Mantra Action:

Leave an hour before you're expected somewhere and explore the area. Meditation occurs in quiet places where your brain has space to relax. Arrive in a space as your best self and enjoy this new experience with a fresh set of eyes.

Mantra Benefit:

Arriving early might seem counterintuitive to "going slow," but when you no longer have the stress of arriving at your next engagement on time, you'll find it easier to explore and find the beauty in the world around you.

Be the change.

Let these words be a reminder that you have the power to transform not only your own experience, but also that of those around you. Throw yourself into it. Positive change is contagious and will catch sparks in the right environments.

Mantra Action:

Always remember to be the change that you wish to see in the world and in your life. When a butterfly enters its chrysalis, it does not simply morph into a butterfly but it becomes liquid, shedding the vestiges of its former life entirely so that it can transform into its true body. Be this change; be something so entire and complete that you can't remember how gravity confined you to the ground for so long.

Mantra Benefit:

Change is the only constant.
Learn to embrace change and you'll be brave enough to take a step to make a change when necessary.

Patience.

Everything worthwhile takes time to reach fruition. Practice patience with others, and with yourself. Be kind with your time. Meet others where they are and not where you think they should be. Have realistic expectations of their capabilities and your own, and do not rush the process. There is nothing that patience, time, and empathy can't resolve.

Mantra Action:
Find a comfortable seat and settle in for a long meditation. As time passes, begin to notice if parts of your stance are uncomfortable. Do not adjust. As your foot falls asleep or your elbow twitches, sit in your discomfort and take deep breaths until the feeling passes.

Mantra Benefit:
When you realize that discomfort is fleeting, you will be more comfortable in difficult situations that will help you grow as a person. Embrace the moment of discomfort and know that it will not last forever.

Let it go.

There it is. You can feel it. You know exactly what it is you're supposed to let go. Perhaps it is a slender thread or even a whole closet full of grievances that will never reach a resolution. Cut the strand, release the tension, and let it go—either because they are too small to effectively grasp and untangle or too big to ever tackle. Do not nurse these petty grievances with gravitas. Holding on to them will only bring you down. Let it go, and you'll find that you're the one who is free.

Mantra Action:

During your meditation, clench your hands into tight fists on the inhale. Clench your muscles. Shrug your shoulders toward your ears. Scrunch your face into pin-point features. Then on the exhale, relax it all. Roll your shoulders down your back. Open your chest. Release the tongue from the roof of your mouth. Unfurl your fingers and let whatever you're hung up on fall to the floor.

Mantra Benefit:

Your brain will follow your physical body if you let it. When you tell your body to relax, it'll send cues to your brain to release the tension as well.

BE
STILL
AND
KNOW.

Quiet truths are hard to discover in loud spaces and with thoughts. Be still and patient with yourself and with everything that life may bring, because being still enables you to know. Know that there is a higher power that is always there for you. I am still, therefore I know that all is well with my soul.

Mantra Action:

Take time to be still, look within, and listen. Allow things to happen in their own time. Stillness is the path to serenity. Be still, breathe, let go, and trust.

Mantra Benefit:

Belief in brighter times is what guides us through the dark.

YOU GOT THIS.

Believe in yourself. Know that you are strong enough to get through anything. You are the only you to ever exist and you're doing a stellar job. Remember that challenges are part of the story. Keep going and never give up. You got this!

Mantra Action:

Practice good posture. Stack the vertebrae of your spine on top of one another and hold your head high as if a string is pulling it towards the sun. Take a power pose, Wonder Woman-style, with your hands on your hips and your feet firmly planted hip distance apart. Let the channels of energy flow through you and don't dump into your joints.

Mantra Benefit:

When you let the channels of energy flow through you, you'll find that confidence will follow. Believe that you are strong, and you'll know that you can tackle whatever life throws at you.

Be
here,
now.

Happiness and calm can be found when you're present in this moment.

Mantra Action:

Ground yourself in the concrete truth of your body. Scan all the synapses in your body and explore the feeling. Start at the crown of your head, move down to your eyelids, cheeks, nose, earlobes, throat, collar bones, shoulders, elbows, knuckles, fingertips. Trace the line of feelings down each rib. How do your hips sit? Are they open or closed? Is there a tingling in your knees? Where does the heat of your limbs overlap? Scan from the top of your head to the tips of your toes, then go back up again to fully ground yourself into your body once more.

Mantra Benefit:

In those moments when your mind wants to be in one place but your heart needs to be in another, bring yourself back to the present moment where you'll find true peace and happiness.

Love

REMEMBER
WHO
YOU
ARE.

Remember that the sky is blue above the clouds. Remember that the seeds you sow in the fall will break through the frosty ground in the spring. Remember that you are not your struggles or your circumstances. Remember that everything you seek is already within you. You are love, you are light, you are peace, you are joy. You're more than a single interaction or decision. You are a fully-realized person. You are bigger than your body, bigger than your thoughts, your past, and your future. Remember who you are.

Mantra Action:

Meditation is the sometimes tedious process of bringing a playful and wandering mind back to a place of stillness. This function of guiding your thoughts to a quiet place will strengthen your mind and ability to think.

Mantra Benefit:

A strong mind is a key component to carving out a spot for yourself. By doing so, you will encourage a more self-aware life.

INFINITE
LOVE

Love is the only universal truth.
Love is simple. Tt needs no explanation.
Love is unconditional, complete, and free.
Love is kindness. Love is compassion.
Love is strength that can move mountains.
Let this be a reminder that you are loved
wholly, truly, infinitely.

Mantra Action:

Unblinking, effervescent, uplifting, and strong, love wants to be shared. Love is infinite and it yearns to be let out. Vent your love to all that lives around you.

Mantra Benefit:

A racing heart. An illuminated brain. Dopamine. Serotonin. Who doesn't love love? Who can truly be whom they're meant to be without love? It is water in the soil, air in our lungs, songs in our ears. Love is meant to be everywhere.

Family is forever.

Family is a circle of strength, love, and support. Whether it's the family you've chosen or the family you've been given, family is love and memories and your anchor for strength. Family is forever, always, no matter what.

Mantra Action:

Talk to your family. Hear their voices. Connect to your past and let it be your present. Tell them often and loudly that you love them.

Mantra Benefit:

By strengthening these bonds, you're strengthening yourself. By loving the people who raised you, you're finding love in yourself.

Be the light.

Bright eyes. Flashing grins. Sparkling personalities. Light wants to burst free from us and out into the world if we choose to nurture it. Tiny fires burn in all our hearts, and when we choose to let ourselves glow, we grow.

Mantra Action:
Shine the light that is within you. Be kind, choose joy, give love. Be the light in your own life, and in the life of others.

Mantra Benefit:
Your light will seek out the light in the world around you.

I am.

These are the most powerful two words, because what you put after them shapes your reality. I am strong, I am brave, I am beautiful, I am hopeful, I am smart, I am hilarious, I am not alone, I am grateful, I am happy, I am enough, I am love, I am worthy. I am.

Mantra Action:

Write it down and say it out loud. You are who you say you are. "I am who I say I am." By saying and writing down your affirmations, you train your mind to believe them.

Mantra Benefit:

Your words and affirmations become your reality. Only say things that you want to be realized in your life.

Choose love.

In every moment of your life, you have the choice to come from love or fear. Choose love over fear, trust in the flow of life, and let love be your guide.

Mantra Action:

Take time to question your fears. Figure out what security they are lacking, and with kindness find ways to nurse them from a state of panic and anxiety into the peace and love that they could achieve.

Mantra Benefit:

By confronting fears rather than avoiding them, life will feel fuller. A whole spectrum of understanding, compassion, and peace will open up to you.

LOVE
YOURSELF

Accept and love yourself with all your beauty and imperfections. Be kind to your body and your soul. Embrace your feelings. Tend to your needs with care and compassion. Only by loving yourself will you be able to truly love others.

Mantra Action:

For every imperfection, complaint, and gripe you have about yourself, give yourself two compliments.

Mantra Benefit:

There is much to love about yourself. By taking note of those things when your mind wanders to an unkindness, you'll end up spending more time uplifting yourself than bringing yourself down.

LOVE AND LIGHT.

May love and light always find you, and may you be a vessel of love and light. Let these powerful forces pull you away from your fears and open you to the understanding of oneness. No matter the circumstances, you will always find a way to do good, be good, and see the good.

Mantra Action:

Send love and light to those you think need it. This can be a specific person or a group of people. When you find a place of calm and quiet, send good vibes to them, and a hope that their day is just a touch lighter and more full of love than usual.

Mantra Effect:

There isn't a cap on how much love and light can be shown, so give as much as you can and you will receive it ten-fold.

All you need is love.

Love is spontaneous. Love is kind.
Love is gentle. Love conquers all.
Choose love, spread love, be love.
It's all you really need.

Mantra Action:

Mentally make a list of every person you love and thank them for the gift.

Mantra Benefit:

Love is just as nourishing for the giver as it is for the receiver. Cherish the loves you have and make sure they know they have your heart, too.

Not alone.

When it feels like you are alone in your journey, remind yourself that you are not. Nothing is forever, and this feeling of isolation will pass. You are worthy and you are loved, even when those feelings seem so far away.

Mantra Action:

Be brave, speak up, reach out, stay strong.
Never give up because it gets better.
Think positive and dwell on possibilities.

Mantra Benefit:

A hundred hands have guided you to this spot, and if you reach out for help, someone will be there to pull you up. See the good and never lose hope because hope writes its own story.

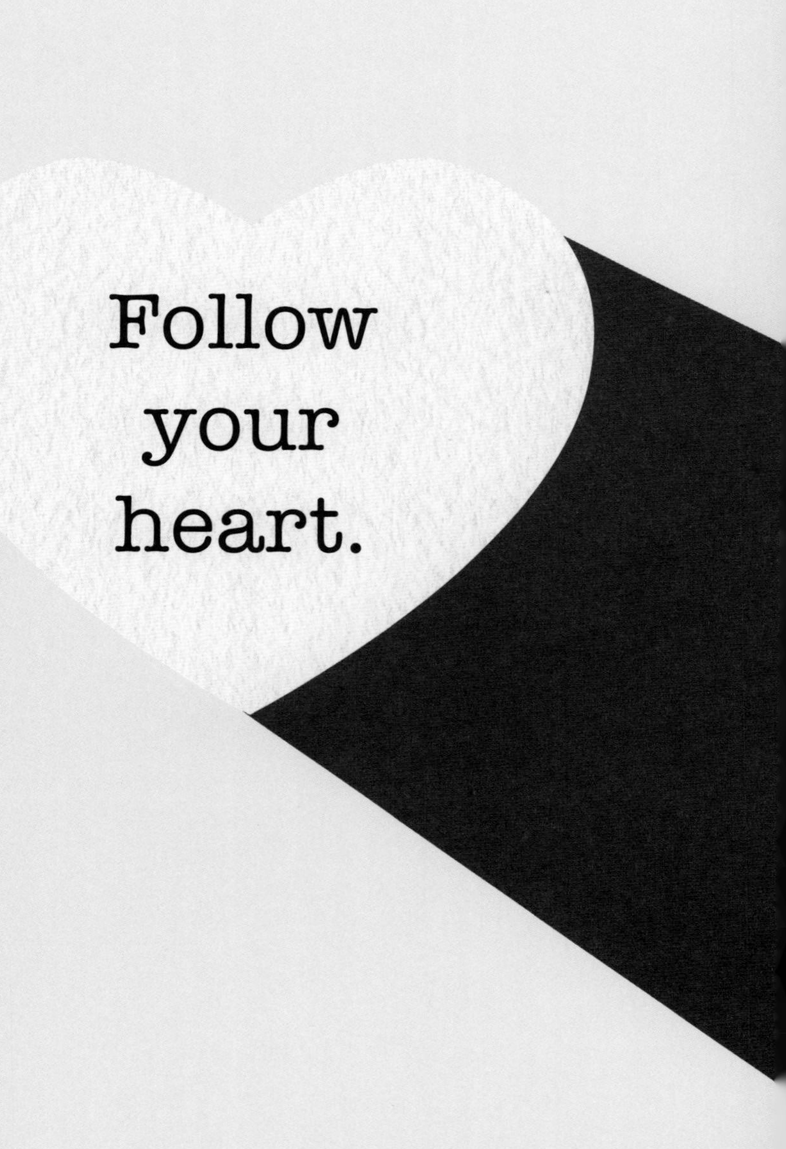
Follow
your
heart.

The heart is a compass that always points north. Notice its whispers and follow its lead. Follow your heart because your heart is your essence, and it will always lead you in the right direction.

Mantra Action:

Intuition is a powerful tool at your disposal. Use it. Guidance from your gut will not lead you astray. Rather than rationalizing a less than desirable choice, take the leap, listen to that little voice, and trust that whatever decision you make is moving you along toward your highest good.

Mantra Benefit:

No more what-ifs. No more daydreams of what could have been. When you follow your heart, you feed your inner child, and you know that you've done all you can to live your most authentic life. When you give the heart what it wants, it blooms.

LIVE
WHAT
YOU
LOVE.

Create a life you love, engage in relationships that you cherish, and do work you are passionate about. Life is to be enjoyed, not endured. So follow your dreams, embrace change, and live what you love.

Mantra Action:

Do something every day that brings you joy. Surround yourself with people who lift you up and do the same in return. Choose a career that allows you to do what you love.

Mantra Benefit:

When you know that it's good to feel good, you will chase that feeling and build your life around it. When you know that life is meant to be lived well and happily, you will attract more wellness and happiness into your life.

Take
care of
yourself.

Always nurture, love, and take care of yourself. Make time to tend to your own mental, physical, emotional, and spiritual well-being. When you're doing well, you will do well in life, for yourself and for others around you.

Mantra Action:

Set aside time in your schedule for yourself. When life is busy and there's not a single moment in it that you can attribute to yourself, begin saying "no" more often. Practice saying "no" to excursions, and experience the joy of missing out so that you will be well rested and better prepared to take care of yourself.

Mantra Benefit:

When you are happy and fulfilled, you can take better care of your loved ones.

I

AM

WORTHY.

This is a gentle reminder to love and accept yourself, and believe in your heart that you are worthy of all good things, now and always. Let in love, let in forgiveness, let in joy. "I am worthy. I am abundant. I am overflowing with love."

Mantra Action:

Decide what matters most to you in life, how you want to live, the kind of relationship you want to have, how you want to feel when you wake up—make note of the big things and the small things. Then decide that you are worthy of receiving these things, believe in your heart that you deserve the best, and work to engrave this into your consciousness every day.

Mantra Benefit:

When you believe that you deserve goodness in life, more goodness and abundance will flow into your life.

Happiness

DREAM
BIGGER.

Life is too short to think small.
Chase your dreams.
Make the impossible happen.
Do something that scares you.
Dare to take up more space, and
go on more adventures.

Mantra Action:

Actively daydream about your perfect life. Try not to think about material possessions, but instead spend time charting out what the most wonderful version of yourself would be spending time on. What's the best possible outcome? Don't be afraid to imagine your biggest dream becoming a reality.

Mantra Benefit:

The amount of work it takes your brain to work on chasing a small dream versus a big dream is the same. You are more likely to be inspired and motivated if the dream is larger and seemingly impossible to achieve.

Live.
Love.
Laugh.

Live intentionally and enjoy every moment. Laugh often. Above all, love unconditionally.

Mantra Action:

Observe your day. Are you present and focused, or are you always multitasking? Whether it's spending time with family or working on a project, you will feel more fulfilled if you do one thing at a time and are fully present in that moment. Do you laugh often? If you don't, how can you bring more laughter into your life? Love yourself first, then love others unconditionally—without expecting anything in return.

Mantra Benefit:

If you strive to do these three things, you can live a more fulfilled and happier life.

FOLLOW
YOUR
BLISS

Do more of what makes you happy. Never let anything or anyone hold you back from your dreams and your hopes. Face your fears, take chances, follow your bliss. Choose to be free. Choose the path with resistance that excites and challenges you. Chase after the childlike wonder that your joy sparks in your heart.

Mantra Action:

Bliss is a high-octane emotion that is not meant to be felt in perpetuity. When you chase after it—tailing it through obstacles—you're just an inch away from catching its heels. Keep your eyes on the prize, the fire churning in your heart, and your feet on the ground.

Mantra Benefit:

Finding your bliss is a marathon, not a sprint. As you track what makes you happy, you'll get better at pacing yourself for a regular dose of joyful moments.

Just dance.

To dance is to be bigger than yourself, bigger than any limitations. Never miss a chance to dance, because dance is the language of the soul. Just dance with all your heart, like no one's watching.

Mantra Action:

A dance is how our body speaks. Break boundaries and cut loose. Cast off the cloak of shame you may be carrying and express yourself through movement.

Mantra Benefit:

Shake the dust from your bones, get out there, and live!

Smile more.

A smile is an action of love that can brighten the darkest of days. Smile because the world always looks brighter from behind a smile.

Mantra Action:

Make it a habit to smile more often. In times when you feel down and want to feel better, try smiling to trick your brain into feeling happy.

Mantra Benefit:

The more you smile, the happier you will feel.

I am lucky.

Have faith in yourself, expect great things, work hard, and seize opportunities. Remember that fortune favors the brave. You are a glorious compilation of luck and hard work, and you'll reach even greater heights with that combination. With every thought and action, you make your own luck.

Mantra Action:

On occasions when you can spare it, relinquish your choices to chance. You're luckier than you think, and this exercise will lead you to new experiences that will help you grow.

Mantra Benefit:

As Seneca said, "Luck is what happens when preparation meets opportunity." When you believe that you're lucky and you prepare for opportunities, you'll be ready to take them.

Think happy.

We spend most of our day thinking. Our thoughts and intentions are the architects of our reality. How we choose to perceive the world, the details that we pick up on, and the relationships that we select to nurture our minds are all at our beck and call. Choose your thoughts wisely. Know that thoughts become words and actions. In the privacy of your own mind, begin the change. Choose positive thoughts and take positive actions. Think happy, and a happy life will follow.

Mantra Action:

Thought transformation is a process. On occasions where you find yourself slipping into less-than-happy thoughts, try welcoming the opposite. "I am worthless" becomes "I am worthy," and "I cannot" morphs into "I can." When you start worrying about worst possible outcomes, shift your thoughts to think of the best possible outcome instead.

Mantra Benefit:

These subtle changes to your thoughts will ripple into your life. By thinking happy, you'll find that little sparks of joy will worm their way into your daily activities. Think happy thoughts and eventually you will be genuinely happy, too.

BE
YOUR
OWN
KIND OF
BEAUTIFUL

Know that you are unique, love what makes you different, and be who you are. Trust your intuition, and hear and speak your inner truth. Know your values, live mindfully. Let go of things that steal your joy, and do what makes you happy. Never compare because we are all beautiful in our own special way. Appreciate and be grateful for what you have and you'll always have enough. This is the key to true peace and happiness. Be your own kind of beautiful.

Mantra Action:

Accept yourself and be who you are. Relish the fact that you are the only one of yourself. See beauty in yourself and in others.

Mantra Benefit:

When you show up as yourself in all your glory, you attract people who will accept you for who you are, and inspire others to be themselves, too.

Optimist.

You see opportunities everywhere you turn, and you act on them. You know that you can, you should, and you will take action to make a change. Believe in yourself, believe in the future. See the good today and believe in a better tomorrow. Trust your decisions and remember that everything happens for your highest good.

Mantra Action:

Practice being an optimist at every opportunity you get. See the best in people, situations, and yourself. The world has so much light to give if only you know how to look for it.

Mantra Benefit:

It's all about perspective. Optimism is a way of life. When you train your brain to see the good, you will see challenges as opportunities and will experience less stress and more bliss in life.

I am blessed.

Blessings take many forms and hide themselves in everyday miracles. Know that when you feel blessed, you start seeing all of the little ways in which life works out in your favor. Count your blessings, not your troubles. "I am awake. I am alive. I am blessed."

Mantra Action:

At the beginning and end of each day, think of three blessings in your life. Make this a daily habit.

Mantra Benefit:

When you count your blessings and find that they are plentiful, your troubles seem much less daunting.

You are enough.

You are strong enough, and you are good enough—and it's not because of anything you do or don't do, have or don't have. You are the only one in your unique circumstances, and you are doing a spectacular job with the hand that you've been dealt. You are important. You are loved. You are enough.

Mantra Action:

When plagued by feelings of insecurity or inadequacy, take time and really think about all of the little things you do in a day. Make a note of your goals and how you spent your time. Feel good about the things you did that you really enjoyed in the moment. Whatever you did, whatever you are, you are enough.

Mantra Benefit:

Nurse your ambitions but find contentment in where you are and where you started from. Celebrate small victories. When you take note of the things that make you happy, you'll find that you have all you need to find a reason to smile every day.

Expect miracles.

Always believe that there is something wonderful coming your way. Know that you are loved and supported. Never give up. Stay centered and unwaveringly on track as you embrace your blessings. Believe that miracles happen. Expect miracles.

Mantra Action:

Manifestation is the practice of wishing and hoping for something so deeply that it comes into existence. First, to manifest a miracle, be clear on what you want. Have something specific in mind, and request it from the universe. Continue working hard on your goals. Believe in miracles.

Mantra Benefit:

Your path will be clearer and you'll have fewer obstacles in your way with this combination of manifestation, hard work, and faith. Once your miracle is manifested, don't forget to graciously accept the gift you've been given.

BLOOM
WHERE
YOU
ARE
PLANTED.

Every experience in life prepares you for the next one. You can't always choose where your roots are set, but you can choose to make the best of every situation. You can control your thoughts, actions, and attitude. While you might not be exactly where you would like to be at this point in your journey, you will get there if you use this opportunity to learn and grow.

Mantra Action:

Always strive to be your best self.
Stay positive, practice gratitude,
and bloom where you are planted.

Mantra Benefit:

You can have roots AND wings, but the latter takes time to grow. Be patient, have fun, and treat yourself and your environment with love and kindness. How you do one thing is how you do everything. Stick to your values, work hard, and show up with grace.

BE TRUE.
BE YOU.
BE KIND.

Live authentically and treat others with the compassion that you yourself would like to receive. In turn, ensure that you treat yourself with this same kindness. It is often easy to fall into the trap of being nicer to other souls than we are to our very own. This mantra is your call to be the shining light that you are meant to be.

Mantra Action:

To be truly authentic we need to practice self-love and self-awareness. Get to know yourself. While you meditate, think about who you are as a person. Kindly take stock of them and become self-aware of the choices you make.

Mantra Benefit:

The journey to self-awareness can be arduous if you haven't already started. Being especially kind to yourself during this process is important if you want to make progress and avoid getting stuck.

Strength

Stay strong.

The last mile is the hardest. When you're weary, burnt out, and barely able to get out of bed let alone be your normal thriving self, remember the heat in your heart when you started. Bring your mind back to when you were excited about this challenge and indomitable in your own mind.

Mantra Action:

Every problem has a solution. Every lock has a key. If you get knocked down, get back up again. When you get frustrated with minor or major catastrophes, take a deep breath, center yourself, and stay strong.

Mantra Benefit:

Your strength is multiplied when you push the envelope. Persevere. Stay strong and know that you can. Remember that you are loved, believe that you can overcome anything, and you will reap the rewards.

She
belived
she could
so
she did.

Let these words be your anchor and your reminder that you have the strength and the will to do what it takes. There is nothing you cannot accomplish if you put your mind and heart to it. Always believe that you can, and you will.

Mantra Action:

When you set a goal, believe in your heart that you will accomplish it. When you believe you can, you will be able to put in the hard work and commitment to reach any goal you set your mind to.

Mantra Effect:

Knowing that you can accomplish any goal you set for yourself is winning half the battle. When you know this, challenges become opportunities and your biggest dreams become possible.

I'M A SURVIVOR.

Hold your head up and keep your heart strong. Remember the battles you have won and the fears you have overcome. Remember the strength and light within you. "I am brave. I am resilient. I will persevere. I am a warrior, ready to conquer. I am a survivor, stronger than I've ever been."

Mantra Action:

When you are going through a rough patch in life, remember your strength and know that you will get through this.

Mantra Benefit:

Knowing that you are strong and that you can get through anything will make difficult times feel a little easier.

Born ready.

Be fearless in the pursuit of your dreams and goals. You are ready for challenges, ready for success. You are ready to face obstacles, ready for opportunities. And you are ready for happiness. Each day is a new opportunity for growth, and you came into this world ready to take them all down.

Mantra Action:

In the moment, if you feel the tingling of trepidation or the brimming edge of doubt, center yourself. Straighten your spine. Close your eyes and tell yourself, "I'm not afraid to do this. I was born ready."

Mantra Benefit:

At the end of the day, being ready is a state of mind. It's a primer for facing all that you go toe-to-toe with. In that moment, you'll be ready, and you'll know it.

Fearless.

To be fearless is to do what scares you, to take a chance, and to make a change. It's to love again and to get back up after you fall. To be fearless is to know your fears but never let them stop you.

Mantra Action:

Do one thing every day that scares you. It's an age-old practice, but take it to heart. It can be new foods, new blocks, new people, or speaking up instead of staying quiet. Try anything that doesn't come as effortlessly as breathing. Face one hiccup a day, and you'll be fearless in no time.

Mantra Benefit:

Fearlessness and courage are primers for bold confidence. The best things in life happen when we are strong enough to face and conquer our fears.

THIS
TOO
SHALL
PASS.

Everything experienced in life, good or bad, is only temporary. Whether you're going through a hardship or surrounded by love and joy, take a deep breath, embrace the moment, and remember that this too shall pass.

Mantra Action:

When meditating, picture stray thoughts like leaves or twigs on a lazy river. They enter your periphery for a time, then go away with little to no resistance. Do not chase them down the bank. Practice the art of letting go and embrace the fact that important thoughts will come back to you.

Mantra Benefit:

Understanding that everything is fleeting allows you to move more freely among the moving parts of the universe.

THOUGH
SHE
BE
BUT
LITTLE,
SHE
IS
FIERCE.

This saying from Shakespeare's "A Midsummer Nights' Dream," portrays the essence of bravery and strength. She will get up whenever she falls. She knows herself inside and out. And she will face challenges with courage and hope. And though she be but little, she is fierce.

Mantra Action:

Know that your ability has nothing to do with your size, your appearance, or your age. Don't put limits on yourself. You are limitless. Let your life mirror.

Mantra Benefit:

It doesn't matter how small or big you are, or how young or old you are—you are here on purpose, you are worthy, and you can do anything you put your mind to.

HAVE
COURAGE
AND
BE
KIND.

Through challenges and triumphs and whatever life may bring, remember that you already carry all that you need inside. Never let anyone dull your shine. Be brave, have courage, and be kind.

Mantra Action:

Stand up for yourself, speak up, be bold, and don't let anyone hold you down. Show kindness at every opportunity you get because—a simple kind gesture or a smile can make a big impact on someone else's life.

Mantra Benefit:

When you take care of yourself and have a strong ground to stand on, you will be able to speak and act with a loving heart.

Trust yourself.

Trust yourself, because you are the only one who knows what is best for you. Listen to your inner voice and trust your intuition. Trust that you have the strength to do what it takes. Trust yourself in your path to truth.

Mantra Action:
When you find it difficult to make a decision, know that whatever decision you end up making will be the right one for you in the long run.

Mantra Benefit:
Trusting yourself makes everything easier. You learn to trust your instincts more, which will lead to better decisions for your highest good.

Strength. Hope. Courage.

You have the strength to conquer whatever life throws your way if you believe in yourself. Take the first step and keep going.

Mantra Action:
Strength, hope, and courage are attributes that are worth cultivating in your life. Make it a habit to be strong, hopeful, and courageous every day.

Mantra Benefit:
Each word reminds you to keep going and that you already have everything that you need inside of you to persevere. Every step takes you closer to your best life.

BE
BRAVE

Remember that bravery is moving forward in spite of fear and challenges. Know that all the strength and courage you need is within you. You are strong, you are brave, and you are loved.

Mantra Action:

In the face of opportunities and challenges, choose to be strong and brave. Never be afraid of failure, because failure is part of any success story.

Mantra Benefit:

Bravery isn't about never being scared or nervous, but bravery is about overcoming the fear when it rears its head. Remember fear is not the master of your fate, you are.

My story
is not over yet.

This is a gentle reminder to stand up for your life and never give up. Remember that you are worthy, you are loved. Know that nothing lasts forever, and this too will pass. Keep going. Your story is not over yet.

Mantra Action:

Everyone's life story has its ups and downs, and so will yours. Whether you're experiencing the lowest of the lows or you've conquered the highest peak, know that this is just a chapter in your story. Keep going, keep writing, keep living. Your story is not over yet.

Mantra Benefit:

Own and know the value of each chapter of your story. Know that you are here on purpose, you are important, and you are making an impact each and every day.

I
CAN
AND
I
WILL.

Remember that you can do anything if you put your mind and heart to it. Dream big, and make your actions as great as your dreams. This is your life, and anything is possible. You can and you will.

Mantra Action:

Visualize what you want from life and meditate on how you can get to that point. Chart your journey step by step. Visualization is more than wishing and hoping. It's setting forth a course to your goals so that your brain can create a map that makes reaching them inevitable.

Mantra Benefit:

When you know that you can reach any dream, you will have more courage to dream big. You'll also have more confidence in your actions and plans to reach your goals.

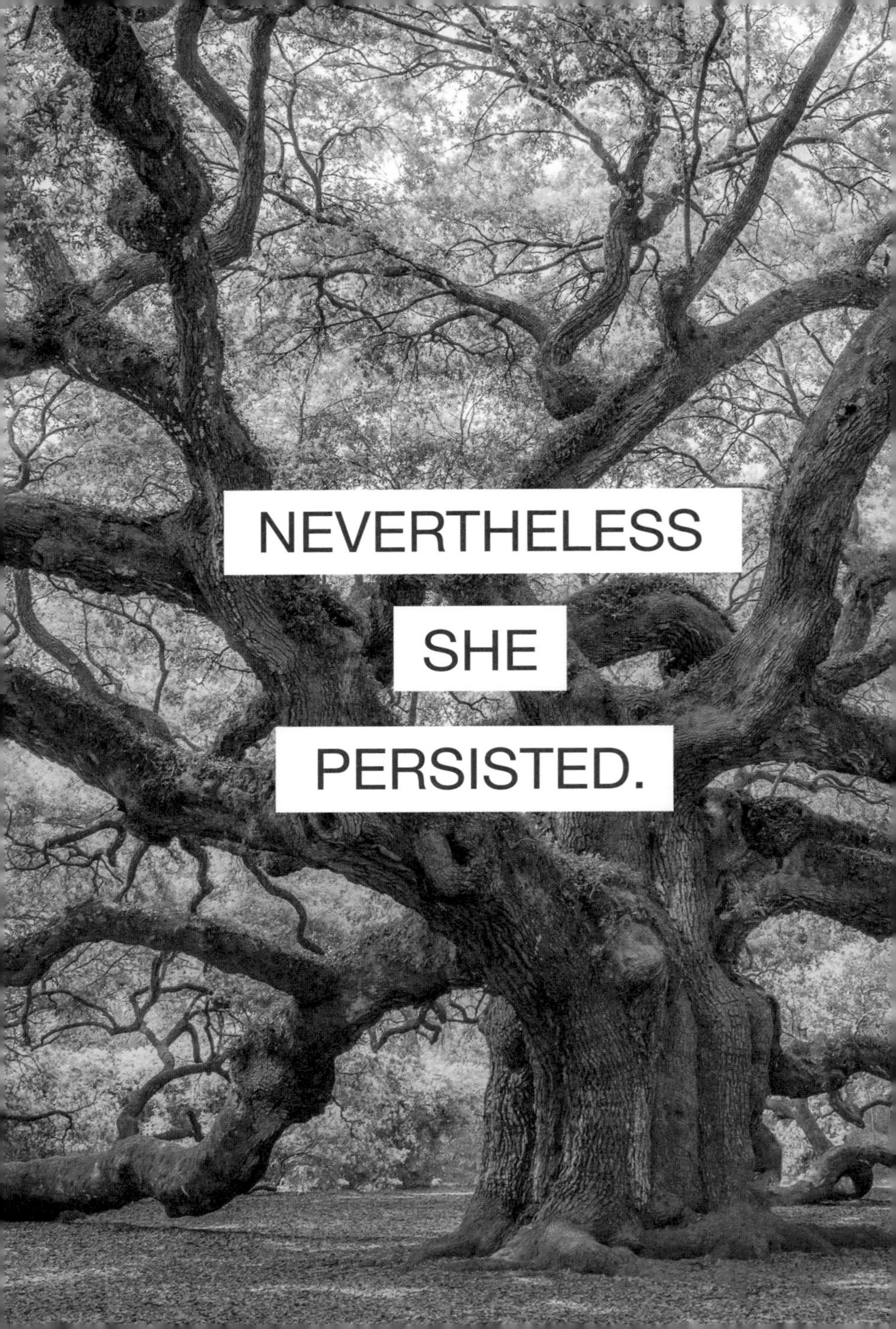
NEVERTHELESS
SHE
PERSISTED.

This is a reminder to keep going, in spite of what might hold you back. It might not be an easy road and there may be bumps along the way, but you will prevail. When everything feels like an uphill struggle, know that the view from the top is worth it. Break the barriers, speak up, stand tall. Be strong, be bold, and never give up.

Mantra Action:

When you feel like you are ready to give up on a goal, perhaps because it's taking longer than you thought it would or it's more difficult than you were prepared for, think of the reason why you started in the first place. Most goals aren't accomplished—not because they are impossible—but because the person gives up too soon.

Mantra Benefit:

You can achieve great things if you don't lose hope and you persist in the face of challenges.

Journey

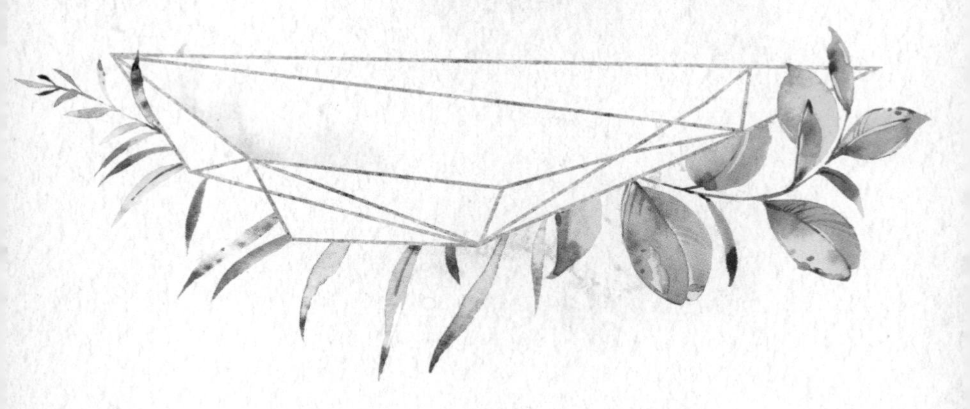

MAKE TODAY COUNT.

The cycle of routines can dull our fire, but each sunrise promises a well of new potential. Remember that your future depends on what you do today. You have a choice to take the steps to make life better in every way. Choose to make this a good day, and choose to make it count.

Mantra Action:

Aim to do something every day that makes your life or someone else's life a little better. For instance, compliment someone; it will brighten their day and make you feel good, too.

Mantra Benefit:

There is beauty, meaning, and opportunity in each day. When you recognize this, your life story will be filled with beautiful memories, laughter, accomplishments, good friends, and happiness.

Remember why you started.

The beginning seems so far away when you're nearing the finish line. Time has passed and you are so tired that the spark and air that ignited this flame are but a tiny flickering memory. Rekindle that flame. Reacquaint yourself with the passion that drove you when this experience was new.

Mantra Action:

Meditate on current projects. Think about what inspired you. If it is a person or place, visit them. Inspiration does not die once you've harvested it. Tap the well, light the match again, and carry on.

Mantra Benefit:

Your reason why you began is stronger than any obstacle or excuse. Let your why fuel your passion and your actions. It may not be easy, but it will be worth it. Remember why you started, stay true to your reason, and keep going until you achieve.

Keep moving forward.

This is a reminder to take it one step and one day at a time. Stay on your path and trust your journey. Never give up, keep going, and keep growing. Keep moving forward.

Mantra Action:

If you are chained down by the past, try removing the clutter from your life to make room for new experiences. Get rid of anything that no longer serves you. Look to the future instead of clinging to the past.

Mantra Benefit:

There's only one way to go, and that's forward. The sooner you realize this, the easier it will be to let go of the past and keep moving into your future.

These are the days.

These are the days that will become memories. Remember to live in the present, enjoy every moment, and make every day count.

Mantra Action:

Do more of what makes you happy. Make memories that you will cherish forever. Remember that family, health, and happiness are the most important things in life. Follow your dreams and don't hold back.

Mantra Benefit:

They are prized. They are few and plenty all at once. You've dreamed of days like these, and now they are yours. Practice gratitude for them, and you'll never waste another minute.

Enjoy the journey.

**Find joy in your life and
cherish every moment,
because in the end,
it's the journey that matters.**

Mantra Action:

Be grateful for experiences and blessings in your life. Commit to your goals, but don't forget to enjoy the journey that takes you to your end goal.

Mantra Benefit:

Everyone is on their own path, but perhaps converging can result in a collaborative happiness. Growth happens at the edge of your comfort zone, and you can find your way there through your own personal experience.

BELIEVE

Everyone has that grumpy voice in his or her head that says, "no." But the most confident among us choose to listen to the quieter voice that says, "yes." Every journey starts with believing, and this belief will keep you going. Believe in yourself, believe in your dreams, and believe that you can.

Mantra Action:

Say "yes" to more and then the little voice in your head trying to pull you down will have to listen. Believe you can do it against all odds. Influential people with a good moral compass need to believe in themselves.

Mantra Benefit:

Belief that there are brighter times ahead is what guides us through the dark.

NOT
ALL
WHO
WANDER
ARE
LOST.

Have the courage to stray off the beaten path and make your own way. Go with an open mind and an open heart. Know that you are never alone. This mantra is your reminder to make your own path to find yourself.

Mantra Action:

Follow your heart and have courage to choose your own path in life. Choosing your own path is a true sign of vision and strength.

Mantra Benefit:

Just because your journey is different than someone else's, doesn't mean that you are lost. When you know everyone has the right and hopefully an opportunity to choose his or her own path, you will be more confident and happier in your own journey.

I am the
master
of my
own fate.

Believe in yourself and in your life's purpose. Know that your thoughts are powerful. Choose yourself. Think positive, see the good, and be strong. Stand up when you fall, take action, and keep moving forward. You are the master of your fate. You are the captain of your soul.

Mantra Action:

You are the protagonist of your story. Choose your path, and the road will rise up to meet your brave soul. Know that you are in control of a lot and that when the world asks you to relinquish control there is either a lesson to be learned or an alternative route waiting to be uncovered.

Mantra Benefit:

When you know that you are the master of your fate, you will become empowered. No one can help you get what you want unless you ask, pursue, and work for it.

One day at a time.

One day at a time is just enough. The past is gone, the future is yet to come. Live in the present, trust the process, and know that everything is going to work out, one day at a time.

Mantra Action:

You only get to live each day once. Seize that opportunity. When you have a goal or a big task to accomplish, break it down into daily steps, then take it one day at a time.

Mantra Benefit:

Overwhelming and never enough, taking it day by day breaks time into pieces small enough to hold and easier to accomplish.

Dream. Believe. Achieve.

Dare to dream big dreams, believe that you can do great things. Keep going until you achieve. If you can imagine it, if you can feel it, if you just believe it, you can do it. Dream bigger, believe with all your heart, face your fears, achieve your dreams.

Mantra Action:

When you set a goal, imagine the best possible outcome. Believe that it is possible and it is going to happen for you. Then work hard, commit, and persist until you reach your goal.

Mantra Benefit:

You need to believe in your abilities and your dreams in order to push yourself through difficult times and failures. When you believe your dream is possible, you will put in the time and effort to make it happen.

DO

IT

ANYWAY.

Do what you feel in your heart to be right. Forgive, because you deserve peace. Do good for no reason at all. Be kind, be honest. Let go because sometimes the right thing to do is the hardest thing of all. Do it anyway.

Mantra Action:

Sometimes you have to do something when you are not ready just yet, or your ego doesn't want you to do it. But you know in your heart that the time is right and that it is the right thing to do. Whether it is forgiving someone or letting go of a relationship, show courage, be strong, and do it.

Mantra Benefit:

It takes strength and courage to take the noble path. Letting go of a closed door will open new doors for you. You will find more strength and peace when you face your fears and do it anyway.

Anything
is
possible.

Cherish your wishes and your dreams. Know that if you can dream it, you can do it. Never be afraid of failure and know that it is another stepping stone. Remember that if you put your mind and heart to it, anything is possible.

Mantra Action:

Think of things that people thought were impossible but that you still accomplished. Remind yourself that little miracles happen every day, and anything can happen with faith and hard work. It is the truth.

Mantra Benefit:

Be an optimist. Know that there are no limits what you can accomplish.

ONE THING AT A TIME.

Focus on one thing at a time. When you walk, just walk. When you eat, just eat. Be present and aware in everything you do. Life is measured not by tasks completed, but by moments truly and fully lived.

Mantra Action:

You don't need to do it all. Do one thing at a time and do it well. Multitasking is a thing of the past. Keep things simple and focus on one job at a time. Delegate what you can, whenever you can. Do less, accomplish more.

Mantra Effect:

You can accomplish so much more if you give all your attention to it. Simple is always better. Keep your tasks, your goals, and your life simple and you'll have more to show for it. You will be proud of every day.

Make it happen.

Your future is what you make it. You will get there if you keep going. This is your life. Today is your day. Get started. Take a chance, make a change, and make it happen.

Mantra Action:

Make the decision that you will be successful in whatever goal it is that you are setting for yourself. If you want to live a healthier life, decide that you can and will accomplish that by taking action every day to make it happen. Once you have made that decision, make a healthy choice every day. Success in anything is but a series of daily habits.

Mantra Benefit:

You are not here to just survive, you are here to thrive. You can make anything happen. Make that decision and do what it takes every day. You will have more to show for it, and you will be proud of every day.

Trust the journey.

Remember that everything unfolds the way it should. Let go, trust, go with the flow, and you will find peace. Trust your journey, and trust the process of your life.

Mantra Action:

When you are dealt a hand that does not seem favorable, ruminate on other times when things did not seem quite so optimistic. Remind yourself that you overcame those obstacles just as you will conquer this one.

Mantra Benefit:

Every path has its peaks and valleys.
Enjoy the hardships as much as what comes easily.

What is meant for you will not pass you.

Trust your journey and let go of expectations. Live your life fearlessly and know that you are supported. Take a deep breath. This is enough. You are enough. What is for you will not pass you by.

Mantra Action:

Life has a way of giving you all you need. Surrender and let it all come to you. Take note of your resources and find pride and gratitude in all that you have. Be thankful and proactive. Use the tools at your disposal. The next time an opportunity skips in your direction, you will be ready for it.

Mantra Benefit:

When we want something we cannot have, it was not meant for us. A better journey will unfold at your feet. Find peace knowing that good things that are meant for you are going to happen.

Live in the moment.

The present is a present, so make sure you cherish the gift and give thanks for it. You're never older than you have been or younger than you will be. Live in the present—free of past and future—and enjoy this very moment that is filled with love, awareness, peace, hope, and freedom.

Mantra Action:

Every so often, as a reminder, carve out a moment with your senses. Focus on as much detail as you can at the most mundane of times. How do the leaves on the trees look? Can you hear anything that remotely sounds like music? How would you describe the feeling at the tips of your fingers? Try not to dwell on the past or future; instead, focus on the now.

Mantra Benefit:

Appreciating the small things in life can make the sparkling moments that much more memorable and special. Fill your lungs with fresh air, drink clear water, and connect yourself back to the ground beneath your feet.

Never give up.

Never give up on your dreams. Never give up on yourself. Keep the faith. Take action. Persevere. Believe in miracles. As long as you are alive, anything is possible.

Mantra Action:
Surround yourself with people who have reached seemingly impossible goals. Read books by and about people who have succeeded in spite of challenges. Learn from them. Persevere in the face of challenges, whether big or small. Train your brain and make it a habit to never give up.

Mantra Benefit:
Anything worthwhile takes time, effort, and sacrifice. Be ready to work hard and never give up. When you are ready and know that challenges are part of the story, you will face them with courage, and you will persevere.

About the Author

Aysel is an entrepreneur and the founder of MantraBand ®, an inspirational jewelry company in Dana Point, California. Born and raised in Azerbaijan, Aysel speaks four languages and understands the power of words to empower, encourage, and enhance life. She's married with two kids, who were the inspiration for her journey in creating products focused on positivity, optimism, and mindfulness. Aysel's jewelry brand can be found at www.mantraband.com. You can also follow the brand on Instagram at Instagram.com/mantraband or on Facebook at facebook.com/mantrabands.